a strange juxtaposition of parts

PRELUDE

I love the way vowels call out to each other
from line to line like soft birds answering
other birds of a feather. Their singing floats
out, spins a fine thread which consonants
with their tiny claws can cling to . . . then

more singing, while consonants edge
around, punctuate, make an architecture
that allows the play of light like intelligence
or sense, though metaphor is never really
tamed but like color, remains wild in the
sight. Its revelations always varying
within the beams of our eyes
 . . . the ancient hum of the voice.

A *Strange* *Juxtaposition*

poems
by

richard pflum

Of   *Parts*

Writers' Center Press
Indianapolis 1995

Acknowledgements

I would like to give credit to those people who have done so much to make this book possible. First, I would like to thank Robert Aull who helped typeset the copy, close read the manuscript, made suggestions for punctuation and continually asked that most important of questions, "Is this really what you meant to say?" And Jim Powell, who has been a believer in and supporter of my work since we first met many years ago. Also Ethel Winslow who reassured the author when he was in a dark time and having many doubts. Last, but not at all least, I'd like to thank Andy Arbuckle whose conversations late into the night about what we might do to save and preserve literature written in English for the coming generations, was such a source of stimulation.

The following poems have appeared in the *Indiannual*:
"Bathtubbing In Tandem," 1984
"Poem With Big Feet," 1988
"Tasting The Winter," 1990
"Inviting The Snowman Inside," 1990
"Machine Gunning The Angels," 1992
In 1992 the name of the publication was changed to *The Flying Island*. "Of Music And Its Earthy Accompaniment" and "Grand Opera" appeared there in 1993, "In The World Of Fancy Divers" in (Spring/Summer) 1994, and "Island" in (Fall/Winter) 1994.

The following poems appeared in *Kayak* #61, 1983: "Poem Beginning With A Line By Walt Whitman" and "At The Concert."

The following poems have appeared in *The Reaper*: "Congratulating The Dead" in #10, 1984, and "Dinner Party" in #12, 1985.

The following poems appeared in the *Arts Indiana Literary Supplement*: "Painters" and "Air Conditioning" in 1989, "Poetry Zoo" in 1991, "Inventing A Ruin" in 1992. In 1992 this publication changed its name to *The Hopewell Review*.

The following poems appeared in *InPrint*, April/May/June 1980, Vol. 1, Nos. 5/6: "On The Death Of Clocks" and "Dozing On A Winter Evening."

"Putting It Somewhere" appeared first in the *Exquisite Corpse*, May--Sept., 1988, and was anthologized in *A New Geography Of Poets* (1992, University of Arkansas Press).

"Swamp" appeared in *Ploplop* 2, 1992; "Shoes" appeared in *Ploplop 3*, 1993 (both by Geekspeak Unique Press, Indianapolis).

The poems "Lepidopterist" and "Me and My Enigma" appeared in *Tears in the Fence 14*, 1995, a publication from Great Britain.

ISBN 1-880649-33-0
© 1995 by Richard Pflum. All Rights Reserved
Writers' Center Press of Indianapolis
Box 88386
Indianapolis IN 46208

Contents vi - vii

DINNER PARTY

When she invited me to her dinner party
how could I tell her the menu would not do?
She had been in such ecstasy about the little
                          watercress sandwiches,
the tiny sugar cookies on silver salvers,
the colorful liqueurs in cordial glasses
and later the fine dark coffee to be served
                          demitasse.
How could I tell her I needed, indeed demanded
so much more than that?
That for me, tireless preparations were the order,
that great slabs of fat and meat
must be hewn like granite from mountains
                          of beef and pork,
that whole orchards must be stripped bare
                          of fruit,
whole dairies put into service for their
                          creams and cheeses,
brewers and distillers made to work three shifts,
bakers, to sweat day and night, rolling out
                          their dough,
the economy of the country to be decimated if
                          necessary,
that rich steaming kettles (carried four men at a time),
might replenish any plate or bowl.

I thought of this when she invited
me to dinner on a Sunday afternoon, and
                          asked me not to forget my poems.

AT THE CONCERT

Teeth are everywhere, wall to wall
teeth: American-beauty teeth
like toothpaste ads, unwholesome
teeth, wolf teeth, but all
smiling mostly at everyone,
trying to be friendly. Trying
to show who they are, big
square blocks of white or
thin-skinned yellow, lipstick
flecked, tobacco flecked. Still,
all pretending to be full sets
even those that are false.

Now everyplace I turn I am walking
on them. They are in my hair,
nipping at my ear, my rear,
my private parts.
The skin of my hand catches
on a fang, my clothes
begin to tear, saliva drips
from the air . . . then, with
everything wet from smiles,
the clatter suddenly ceases
and music begins.

INVITING THE SNOWMAN INSIDE

On the lumpy white lawn he glares at us,
seems frozen to our polite overtures.
We see he lacks a certain social polish
though we sense a strength in him,
a certain purity of resolve.
We determine that deep inside he
must contain reservoirs of character,
that love would not be impossible for him,
and so . . . invite him indoors.

Since he is a little stiff
we help with wheelbarrow and shovel.
Once the door is closed we seat him
before the fireplace,
offer him cognac and apple strudel.
Here, he listens politely to our
casual conversation but is
strangely reluctant to speak.
When we question him about his ambitions
and prospects for the future,
he shrinks down into the sofa,
tears well up in his eyes,
he perspires profusely, his hat
sinking down to his nose.

After a short time his muffler is soaked
and his carrot nose has fallen to the floor,
His hat, now beside him, half fills
with water from puddles on the cushions.
When the wet coals of his eyes roll
across stone to the grate of the cheery
fireplace, they flare brilliantly
. . . pop like popcorn.

POEM BEGINNING WITH A LINE BY WALT WHITMAN

"Look for me under your boot soles,"
or anywhere the sun strangles sad animals
and we nibble meekly on their bones.
Wherever stones cry like sirens
in conglomerate cathedrals,
look for me in the headlines
or on the sporting page,
in the weather reports,
under the headstones of famous
bricklayers and acrobats,
in the fashionable patios of the poor,
restaurants of the dyspeptic,
whorehouses of the celibate.

You will see me there, the red
ghost of a round man on roller skates,
celebrating his newest escape,
playing soccer with the moon.

SWAMP

When I stop to think about it, getting
back to the swamp is all I've
really wanted. The cities are just
too crowded, with their green ataxias
and Technicolor grease pits,
with their mobilized armadillos
and children playing "autopsy"
under the blue triangles of
Bulgarian cafeterias. Sentimental
to say this I suppose, but swamps
have so much more glamour.
You can drive there with your
hungry wolf to gnaw on a stick or
stone, and play "fudge" in the primal
ooze, or doze in Nature's own
contagious bathtub, dream of
Salamanca and Carborundum,
and other brilliant things.

Still, I'll probably have to remain
where I am, my tricycle having
developed square wheels and these
crutches now worn down to my knuckles.
While Splot, my wolf, would rather
run down the neighbors who live
on the next lot anyway, than seek
the more novel quarry hiding under
abandoned refrigerators. And I
myself would rather forage in
the familiar dump of domestic petards,
where brown gravy spills so lasciviously
over the pink, glowing new potatoes.

CHAOS

Chaos follows me, an incendiary threatening
to erupt at any moment. Always I struggle
to put things into order, straighten
my life, my room, my desk, bookshelves.
But it follows me, a mugger with
brass knuckles and matches in his hip pocket.
And friends are too shy to come close.
They know. They smell the stench of chaos
like gasoline on my clothes, see the catsup
stains like blood on my shirt.

My only victories against it are hard-won
and incomplete, as I wrestle with
my keyboard trying to make a deadline
and my screen goes black and the disk
is stuck in its slot, while the cartridge
has popped out of its printer
and smudges my hands and face.
Then the juice from my hamburger smears
all over everything else
as I slobber over my poems in a fury
and they spit back.

No wonder my friends ask, ''what's
the matter?'' when they see me approaching
on the sidewalk and sense that small black
cloud hovering just behind my shoulders.
They stay put on the curb when I try
to cross the street and am almost hit
by some crazy driver who yells,
''watch where you're going, asshole,''
and I snap, ''up yours too, buddy,''
and move on, hard.

AN UNEXCEPTIONAL DAY IN OCTOBER

The birds are flying south again
over this house I've never lived in
but is so full of treasures and mementos.
In my bedroom the unmade bed
is still warm from where I didn't sleep
and in the shower a beautiful woman
is singing, thinking of me
though we have not touched,
much less made love.

I start to dress for I am naked.
Look for the stiff unworn shoes
which I always put on first.
On the wall photos of my parents
reproach me.
We have never been introduced,
for when I am here
they are always someplace else.
I hope one day we become friends
and that these new lead suits they
send me, seamless but with
breathing holes, will fit
should I chance to put one on.
And that the woman rinsing
her body in the bathroom
will approve . . . smile,
should we meet clandestinely
at the supermarket.

SETTLING IN

All my friends are building new rooms
for themselves, around the rooms
they live in. They are chinking up
the cracks, sealing out the starlight,
checking for leaks. I politely decline
when they invite me inside . . .
though their lighting fixtures
are almost as good as the sun, and
their central air conditioners compare
favorably with the North Wind, and
the huge speakers make fine imitations
of bird songs, and though I know
I will miss our warm conversations,
slipped-in between the hottest soaps
and the latest rock videos.

I ask them why they are doing this.
What are they preparing for? They tell
me, "for the great discontinuity to come,
which will be a time of much activity
though no one will actually move
but sit securely in their sealed-off rooms
growing wings perhaps, or translating
the night's ambiguous signals which will
arrive continuously from the outside."

I ask them what is going to happen and
they say, "nothing," and that this is
the best possible thing, though "nothing"
might seem to be a problem for some
and might require a great deal of fixing.

I tell them that someday the diggers
are sure to come and demand explanations.
That they will probe the machines
(probably still running) and find they
are just empty cardboard boxes.
That they will taste the blue medicines
we prescribe for ourselves and find
them savorless and without effect.
Examine the bookcases and discover
the expensive bindings contain only
sawdust and salt, that the thick collections
of recordings and tapes when played
will hiss back only the negative beats
of some giant ineffectual heart.

My friends say, "yes, but that will be
                              their problem."

THE NEED FOR LOUD MUSIC

"Turn it down!" she screamed over the din.
"But Mother Goose," I replied,
"no picture is just blue or red," and
I continued my jangling on the autoharp,
singing sweetly in the lower registers
of my rich *basso falsetto* while the clocks
roared like lions and the puppies went on eagerly
eating my breakfast from under the ottoman.

"Turn it down," she frothed, and began beating
my pate with her Chippendale rolling pin
while the puppies fought like gladiators over
the remains of my six-month-old socks, still
unhappily in tatters on my cold- bitten feet.
"Turn it down, turn it down," she bawled.
"But Goosie," I answered, "how can you deny me
my butter and my bread with each note worth
a thousand pictures, and even the softest notes
from *La Gioconda* turn you on your head."

And she became a tornado in lace, pirouetting
in flimsy party things while all our children crept
out from under her oceans of black hair, singing
like a cloister of crows, but she spun away from them,
flinging the rolling pin to the stars (a new
constellation seen only after the winter solstice).
And she whirled about as I now plucked
the strings of a *pianoforte* with goose quills
in a gentle tune, when the puppies brought down
a crash of pans and utensils from the scullery kitchen.

And so I grabbed a convenient handle from the floor
and cut off both her ears with a butcher knife,
threw them up to heaven to join the rolling pin.
Now I must sing twice as loud for her to hear
as we sit amidst broken antiques and the mythic
beasts our pets and children have grown into,

reminisce sweetly about those extravagant times.

QUANDARY

Because it was the *cantabile* of spirit
that I craved, the world disturbed me.
None of the scenic views remained pure,
the detritus of my own rich breakfast
polluted the flow of brooks and faucets.
The cattle for my breakfast burgers
continued to graze lovingly in my bathtub
though I scrubbed and scrubbed until
my hide was raw as feathers
or the scales of untutored sopranos.

Perhaps it was stroke that I was really
drawn to: stroke, soaked in a mixture of
eggs, bread crumbs, and palm oil, everything
gooey with low-density cholesterol.
If not stroke perhaps the even more radical
coma . . . slurpy with rich chocolate syrup.
Oh yes I can see it now, the nurses
surrounding me in my private room
sprinkling chopped peanuts on my dome
while the intern hurries back to the supply
room in his mad search for whipped cream.

But what good would the treatment
have done me anyway with all those sweet
people dying in Kansas and other places.
What I really, really needed was a bell
and the *cantabile* of spirit to go with it,
not the purple ambulance and the driver
with his spear, not the black rhino horn
dusted parasympathetically into my plebeian
soup, not the hundred Chinese acupuncturists
punching me up to heaven or wherever.

I could have dispensed with the services
of those technicians who scurry from floor
to floor carrying their angioplastic balloons
and confetti, and those dietitians, so aroused,
who follow excitedly, all hectic-pink
and creamy in their anorexic glow.

LATER,

I wanted to go back and so I walked.
But when I got there, there was nothing,
not one familiar stone or tree stump.
And when I asked the next-door
neighbors what had happened they
could only say how sand was
beginning to drift over the property
line and clutter their driveway,
that two weeks ago a truck had
stopped and taken the boards
that made up the walls along with
all the shingles of the roof, that the
apple trees had also been collected
along with every blade of grass
and even the stray squirrel
who sometimes ventured into the yard.
That the inhabitants of the house
had left with their arms full,
saying nothing. That my dog,
looking apprehensive at first, finally
climbed into the truck cab with
the others and they had all driven away
posed like statues.

Now unusual things were happening like
rain refusing to fall behind the fence,
and at night strange men dressed in black
scatter what looks like salt from
bags they drag around the yard . . . while
the wind makes hushing sounds
when it blows across the barren lot
through what seems
to be invisible shrubbery.

POETRY ZOO

This poetry stuff is for hairy angst-mutterers,
I think, or other lambent and dullish smerds.
There are so many other animals, and zoos
are never properly equipped for poets like me:
no retractable incompositors, no flied French
horns in incomparable Japanese goopy sauce,
not a single green embulus dispenser.
I pant to think of all the other animals
they take but not me, like the spiral shaped
peanut snipe, the worsted wet rat musher,
the circular amblivion, even the cool-Fab
with its small undistinguished leather fluut.

Oh! to have been the gum-running, rave scatcher
under the eyes of these obvious snoots, that the
world might not count me as resigned, when I grovel
in the vapid offices of these yellow fowl-mouthed
                              degenerate groan farks,
attempt redress from their scrimped, dung-beslimed
ledgers, find my own clean bright space, even while
they gambol beneath their lurid fumeries of gas.

OF THE NOVICES

I have nothing but tears for these bumbling, asphalt
comedians, for the world is without remorse when it
presses their elbows into their sides, leaves little
room as they attempt their difficult act: the juggling
of precious artifacts, these infinitely spiraling,
deliciously pulpy hearts of artichoke, the cosmic
eggs, which if broken spill a sweet milky sap not
only over both their shoes but over the universe, too.
And then there are those other more recondite yet
flashier tokens: silver meat cleavers, sticky door knobs,
glass eyebrows looking like sugared millipedes,
everything that wants to float over a raucous, bloated,
yet new and still strangely verdant continent.

Here they are, after having traveled from a great
distance at much personal expense, and at an even
greater critical risk to their own well-being. Salt
streams down my chilblained cheeks when no one will
support them, for they are shouted down or ignored
by those who would blaspheme our common origins,
those who crudely serve themselves *always* first,
who long ago lost that common touch which these
new ones have in such great abundance. And so the
old ones might say, "let us be rid of them, they with
their grass-lined ambitions. Let us push them straight
through their beds at midnight so that they might
never be heard from again. We can easily usurp their
profiles and portfolios, fill out the requisitions,
sign all the proper forms in triplicate.

"For we need no laughter except what we can provide
for ourselves: a belly flutter or two perhaps, a tickle
in the groin, maybe even the hilarity of a heaved-up
breakfast in a large public amphitheater or in some
cozy, warmly-appointed room where a saucy, freckle-
bottomed, topless dancer is awaiting a windfall of
fuzzy Indian clubs and over-ripe bananas. And though
these eager intruders might seem reflections of our-
selves in our best form, we cannot afford for our names
to be reassigned to them. Wait while they collect all
the brass animals and amulets, the grandfather clocks,
other bright suburban ephemera which we need so
badly if we are to furnish the charming Bavarian
villas we have built so close to the sea.

"We must take the initiative now, while they are still on
unsteady ground, make use of our tiny red hatchets, filet
their delicate, new white bones, their soft blue veins."

IN THE WORLD OF FANCY DIVERS

I do belly-flops, expert belly-flops,
patented ball-smashers, almost empty
the pool with ferocious displacements,
fill air with coruscating prisms
that wet the very sunlight.
And those around the edge either curse
or wonder at such clumsiness, and
why I do it over and over, and what
about the pain, or the joking anger
from those smoothies who knife
the surface with such apparent ease:
whose only fear is that some miscalculation
might send them sprawling . . . flat
into the water, drenching the illusions
of both fans and judges alike
with myriads of chlorinated drops.

LEPIDOPTERIST

In its continuing deception, my own brash but cagey char-
acter eludes me though I chase it around everywhere. It flutters,
a butterfly knowing of its pursuer, obstinately refusing to settle
into one pose or focus in an otherwise perfectly motionless
landscape. Still, I often think of it as something else,
perhaps a lead weight that first hangs its arms
around my neck like soluble water wings
then walks briskly away on stilts through
the eddies of a quiet but ever deepen-
ing pool, a pool whose surface is
only occasionally disturbed by
  the smash of a crowbar. Yet,

    since I walk on water . . . although very awkwardly,
      I know I am closing in. For my dis-
        guise is almost picture-perfect as I
    lurk about in my blond wig and cigar, a large zirconium

  ring on my right pinkie, and of
course the great vanadium bracelet en-
circling both the pierced lobe of the left ear and
the left nostril of my false nose. Once it is caught I
will have exclusive rights, for no one else really needs it
or even understands its significance. And so, having had long
experience with this beast, I pursue with a cool diligence and in
an altogether most exacting and skillful manner (one might even say
"professional" although I *do* lack the formal education and certifi-
  cation which would validate this claim—in the eyes of most fist-
    ular Academics and piebald Public Officials, anyway).

PUTTING IT SOMEWHERE

Let's put it anywhere but here.
Let's dump it in Indiana
or in Utah, put it under the lake
where no one will find it.
Let's dump it in Vermont or Maine,
or in Montana or Washington State
under a mountain where earthquakes
maybe won't shake it loose,
or on the bottom of the sea
where the fish might love it, grow
corpulent, maybe sprout three heads
and sharp teeth.
Or on the sun, let's shoot it to the sun.
Hope the sun will enjoy it
or be too far away to spit it back
if the taste is really bad.

Let's give it to Canada wrapped up
in green ribbons like a gift; they certainly
have space in which to put it, or maybe
to Mexico wrapped in corn-shuck disguised
as tamales . . . so hot and so tangy.
I'm sure we can put it somewhere.
We have clever people who have studied
in universities: they understand
its strange light and unearthly warmth.
They have given the information
to important men in ties and white shirts
who make green money and give us jobs
and hospitals, who send out employees
in huge trucks to pick up our trash
every Thursday morning.
They will know what to do with it:
they deal with it all the time.

They have machines where it comes out
one end while fresh dollars in very
large denominations come out the other.
They are very clever people.

Today it is up to our ankles;
tomorrow it will be up to our knees.
We can feel it itching inside our socks,
squishing between reddened toes.
We were given dominion over it;
there must be a place to put it.
God must have provided a place . . .
maybe in your backyard?
Certainly not mine.

ISLAND

It begins first underneath, with some congested
volcano clearing its throat, then sediment and ash
layering up through water and the sand heaping
in from the waves. Later very small sea creatures
crawl onto and around the surface, die and leave their
skeletons so the land becomes higher, spreads out
and is a place to walk on. Then plants spring up in
small clusters from seeds that have floated in or
have been dropped by migrating birds, and after
thickening, push forward, branching and finally
close in, together. Now one must work to walk from
one end of the island to the other, for tiny seedlings
have become a tangled jungle that resists intrusion.
At night, sounds of its wispy conversations
with itself are carried on the wind.

It is then I know something is here besides trees
and the small birds on their way to someplace else.
That there is another animal on the island, though
no ship has ever dropped anchor here, and from
anywhere is much too far for a jungle animal to
swim. Sometimes I will see it in the moonlight
peering out between matted branches and leaves.
But if I look up too sharply, everything moves
quickly, protectively, silently closes. And
where it was again fills with lush tendrils.

Though I have guessed what it might be, the essential
mystery of how it came and why, remains, being what
it is: devious, obscure, and mostly wild, not easily
distinguished from the rank home where it lives.
Being almost invisible in its camouflage of dark lines.

OTHERS

They want in, step on each
others' hands and feet, jump
on top of the pile, push against
the gleaming gate, hollering,
clawing, making obscene gestures.

Those inside are calm,
touch cheeks and foreheads
to the cool chromium bars,
touch tongues to fine cedar oil
that coats jewel-like hinges
and hard iridium locks.
They look down past the shining
grill-work of the floor
to the spotless pit below them . . .
so white there are no shadows,
then up to the sky's unreal blue.
They work with their eyes trying
to see the cables that suspend them,
the source of the heat which warms
their nakedness, those exquisite
and ultra-thin filaments
which lower food and drink.
But it is all fruitless and so,
the perfect quest.
Their hands snatch quietly
at nothing when nothing passes.
They invent, retell again and again
their fabulous history
(the myths of the golden heart,
where their story ends).

Later, the others outside go away
to sleep and to mate: find
energy for tomorrow's
fresh assault.

GETTING THERE

The women of the 747 are singing
just to me alone.
Singing as they mix drinks
I will pay for both now and later.
They are also smiling as they
hand me magazines about
nude sunbathing
in the south of France.
Soft tresses just touch my cheek
when they bend over
to check my safety belt,
their pink lips whispering
of the fantastic things
we might do together
in oxygen masks and life jackets.

They brush my shoulder and ear
with undulant sweet bottoms and hips
as they move up and down the aisle.
Then suddenly they close around me,
singing the Brahms *Liebeslieder Waltzer*.
The plane, Lufthanza perhaps,
swings in its beautiful circles.
I am enchanted, floating through clouds
of lavender and edelweiss.

When I wake up we are in Indianapolis.

GRAND OPERA

Then there is the plot of the real universe: with its
insistence on dispersal, if not wholesale, then at least
in the long haul to nowhere when no one is ever heard
from again because time itself is always vanishing.
And so there is the chaos of the body, with its snivel-
ing demands of order as it tries to wrap things up.

Ah so tidy . . . when it decays into its own skeleton,
or earlier, its fumbling attempts to become *one* inside
some *other*. Still the fragrance is nice wouldn't you agree,
on this particular late spring evening, with this labor
of love being performed so exquisitely? The stage: a garden
full of freshly opened roses, the moon, a swelling orchestra,
the tenor, the soprano, both buck-naked at their aria.

ME AND MY ENIGMA

He follows me everywhere
and people are sometimes shocked,
particularly at formal parties
where young women squeak
when something disturbs their thighs
under the dinner table.
Or at a literary cocktail bash
as the stylish hostess is about
to sit and before her bottom
touches bottom, everyone knows
where the cold nose of my
enigma is about to sniff.
And in bars where couples dance,
bodies blending in ethanolic bliss,
there my enigma is, pushing
between them, his hot breath
smelling of garlic and root beer,
surreptitiously licking spit curls on
the back of some graceful neck.

And at the supermarket, at heel yet
unabashed and in a carefree prance,
he follows me as we enter automatic
doors. There, the store manager is
at a loss, especially when he observes
us at the meat counter and a feminine
hand reaches across to caress the sirloin
marked-down on sale then pulls
back to find her fingers wet from my
enigma's appreciative tongue . . .

sunny benevolence smiling up at
her from his fuzzy head, as panting,
he awaits some token of her regard.

Yet should anyone confront him:
call him by name, chuck him
under the chin, say he's cute,
pretend they care, he will quickly
retreat behind the nearest bush,
or hide with his nose in
an old boot under the stair.

A HUNGER AFTER FEASTING

In the beginning I was content being near, blush-
ing in her warmth, breathing from her flower-
rich breath. This before knowing a muskier, more
intimate odor, maybe from the lovely valley between her
breasts, or perhaps from holier land, much lower.

We had wanted to step out into cool evening air
just to sit, talk there of sad nostalgic things when
suddenly our tongues were mute, at an impasse
between the other's lips. And though it might have
been less wanton, more tender to have walked,

lingered a bit on the sun-glazed bridges just fading
into dusk, huddled close, listened even closer to
mockingbirds in the darkening trees, our heat (in
hot pursuit) had already overtaken us, and we
were beside ourselves . . . so quickly on top of

each other, first as groaning, ecstatic combatants,
finally as the sweetly wasted, stunned casualties
in her exploded bed. We are both exhausted yet
growing hungry for food when she says, "but I must
have love." I agree as we slowly get up, stumble,

our feet tangled in sheets, our thighs still glued
against one another. Beneath the kitchen table my
hand is casual as it finds the softness under her smooth
knee. After opening up the clam dip I had asked for,
she presses me hard . . . for the pumpernickel.

BATHTUBBING IN TANDEM

Let us gargle moonlight in the
                    bathtub of our dreams,
blow lilac bubbles with our streamlined arses,
          wash between our ivory toes with
                    spongy soapy fingers,
pluck the silver hairs (retain the gold) from
                    pubic nests and underarms.

Let us get our navels clean, clean
     of the Elysian lint of boxer shorts and
                         frilly Parisian skivvies,
raise the continents and archipelagoes
               then let them sink,
polish pale pink peninsulas
                    into ruddy tumescence.

Let us think of lovers coupling, Snow White
          under her sappy slick Prince,
all dripping in the foamy moonlight . . .
               the bathtub a gondola for two
(flowers floating in the effluvia of
                    Pompeiian bathrooms,

soft-scented tissue gyrating
                         on its roller
just waiting to be squeezed).

OF MUSIC AND ITS EARTHY ACCOMPANIMENT

I've always wanted to swim in oceans of sopranos, yes.
Sleep on beds of ballerinas, oh yes.
Stretch in their tight violin strings.

Wanted to glow in the blue arc-light
of eyes, smile back with
the white eveness of pianos,

reverberate like the bones of saxophones,
be spit from the brash spittoons of brasses,
clutched by knees of the voluptuous red-haired cellist.

Just to live, live in the crushed velvet of cases,
in the starch and black of midnight tuxedos,
within the snap and zing of luminous batons.

nuzzle the heaving décolletage
of those exuberant soloists, dancing
legs stretched high above delicate crotch.

Oh yes, such music is a miracle
of muscle, strings, the vibrating membranes of the lips,

astounding blows on the kettle drums,
the rampant hair, *appassionato*,
falling in all directions.

PAINTERS

Today I know the passion of the painters: when
light pours through open windows onto roses in a cool
enameled vase, when air hints of varnish from a warm sun-

washed, walnut endtable, and a blue radiance softens these
floating white curtains. Today I could almost live
without words, let this fine weather lead to a

bright chaos of studio clutter: brilliant
greens, vermillions, ochers, squeezed from tubes,
odors of linseed oil and turpentine, new canvases stretched

and primed for all intensities of color. There, apply my
own light, wet and thick from a lavish palette.
Taste this sweet, salty, palpable world

of surfaces, the promiscuous tongues
of my brushes spelling "yes" over everything.

THE FABLED LANDSCAPE OF ARCADY

Brown shadows of a sparse but brilliantly
green herbage, an enthusiastic yet temperate
wind over an almost frigid turf, make picnics
here quite unusual, prompt the musicians
to open French windows and step out onto
the terrace where the light is so fine, so dramatic,
it reminds us of good dreams. Here, where air
is refreshed by the aromatic breathing of pines
and cedars, where the sound of far-off rushing
water blends pleasantly with any music the
musicians decide to play: where you can stand
quietly alone on the plain with the shrubs
and trees and allow your body to sway into
the wind's seductive pass so that suddenly
you are energetically encompassed, become
a dancer who at any moment will be joined by
the most graceful and beautiful of partners.
Here, where if there is the hint of a mist in
the air and your cheek is brushed by a cold kiss,
you will be drawn down to touch your tongue
to the moss-cushioned rocks along the path:
those pearling their single crystalline drops
into ampoules of the purest radiance.

But it is the light which gives this place
its glow, though the season is without a name
and is always changing. For the light here, with its

strange delineation evokes, however implausibly,
(as in a black and white photo) every nuance of
hue and color. Then on looking out over terraces
toward alien distances or up to visible beams
falling down from amber-edged clouds, one
finds the familiar is still very close: that a credible
lightness of gravity natural to this region so
eases the limbs, one might walk for miles
and miles. While the soft figure you approach,
whose quiet hand and bright face have just
become recognizable, who has slipped
around the hedge to linger in a grove of
newly washed lilac, is the one you will love.

DOZING ON A WINTER EVENING

The bright sign of the fire
is on my face
and I am half asleep
in an easy chair.
At my feet a green log
sizzles up the chimney.
Something is at play
in the flames,
a token from my life perhaps,
a warm song on bubbling air.

I dream the pungent smell
of spring buds on a maple tree
while my bones store heat.
Above, the feet of the wind
are ticking at the roof
and beside me the window
is frosting up.

It is an evening in late December;
six o'clock has come.
Outside, the trudging darkness
makes blue footprints on the snow.

INVENTING A RUIN

I have already bought the land, cleared it
of boulders and overgrown vegetation. Bulldozers
moving back and forth have smoothed out the ground.
Soon trucks will bring the splintered wood,
cracked stones, jagged plaster board and the
simulated Grecian columns. Then movers will unload
the shabby furniture with my personal things:
like the hypo-stained photos to be hung on crumbling
walls, my spavined easy chair and magnificent
mildewed couch to go into the living room, and all
my rotting books to be stacked in rough piles
in the bombed-out library around the awkward
grand piano that bows so precariously before me
on two legs begging for a *coup de grace*.

And I shall truly be myself there,
dressed in the ragged costume of legends,
under a roofless sky, beside hard stones
of a blackened fireplace.
In time ivy will climb the newly weathered
ramparts and people will arrive by bus to visit
and to gape, project what once had stood . . .
imagine its past glories, and almost eagerly
anticipate new disasters that are yet to come.

But I shall be happy just sitting half-revealed
in this all- rewarding present.
One, whom some might almost take to be
the hero, or at least his statue,
under this cold electricity of stars.

HOW TO SLEEP IN A HEXAGONAL BALLROOM

First have the band start playing
either something by J. Strauss the Younger
or Ferrucio Busoni.
Then put all your winter clothes on,
particularly remembering the parka
you inherited from your great-great-Uncle Ed
who was with Amundsen on his
dash to the pole in 1910.
Later you may take this off
but not until you've danced the mazurka
with the woman in purple clogs.

When you have finished this, drink a liter
of ginger-beer imported from the Czech Republic,
then a pint of birch-beer from the Canadian
provinces, follow with 500 milliliters of genuine
Ukrainian vodka imported from Kiev.

Now you may sleep. Lie down in the middle
of the floor, the dancers circulating
in ever-decreasing circles around you.
Cast your eyes on the hexagonal chandelier
above you and think of snow while light
emblazons its rainbow on your forehead,
while graceful feet of the eternal dancers
spin into effigies of pink glass.

A SCHOOL FOR BRANDOS

Start with the well-deliberated drools then
the nose excavated for its green scalloped
scroll (both solid and semi), the scratch of
the funky crotch, the lardy diet, the tongue
tangled behind the bicuspids and the tangoed
tale of a well-buttered bumptious but bitter
broad's bum. Then the funeral, the wife's
sticky corpse with its obvious inability to
speak. Notice her epoxied lips like the frozen
pistons of a burned-out Harley, his shaking
snakeskin epaulets on ovoid shoulders, a
taste for *injuns* (Western) and Indians
(Eastern), for Fletcher Christian's tropic isle,
the brown booty, the flower-scented Tahitian
aureoles. Heaven is a long way from Omaha,
longer from the Actors' Studio, California
kitsch, and the black heart of Nam . . . Mr. Kurtz's
carnal congregation licking the toes of the
Buddha which he would become, which he wants
so very much to become. So what anyway, no
sacrilege here. Hell! the Buddha would approve.

ONE FOR BUK

for Charles Bukowski (d. March 1994)

Up for my baby after a great day at the track, the
scotch eyeing me with its amber stare from the glass,
a late quartet on the stereo and me at the ready
waiting for 10 o'clock when she said she would be here.
Would ditch her old man at some boring party up in the
Hollywood hills so she could bring me her sweet little
Stradivari body and we could make lovely fiddle music
                                on that thing of hers.

We were both drunk when we met at a literary gig
I was involved in, maybe she won't remember. But I'll
never forget those tight bluejeans welded around her
memorable ass and knowing right away that something
wonderful might just be coming my way. Though if 12
comes and she's not here, still the day won't be a total
loss, with that nag coming in at 8 to 1 in the last race,
and me with a glass of Cutty in my hand and old
                                Ludwig on the stereo.

SWEPT UP BY BELLS

for William Stafford (d. 1993)

More like a sudden rough wind in mid-afternoon
calm: this clangor of old beliefs
swirling through sunlight in a courtyard paved
in circular patterned cobblestone,

an anchored castle floating there, high
above the small cries
of children and pigeons

and these iron voices of angels
hammering out gold
all around.

LISTENING WITH OTHERS

Music comes, a lit candle
carried in the dark.
And so I am with company;
a hand touches my shoulder,
leads me first down
empty hallways, then outside
through half-ruined arches
to a formal garden.

As always, the sky
is dark blue and
the sun setting,
when this music comes.
Still, a warm breeze
from the south is there
with its scent of
spices and apples,

and across the water
the moon is rising.

IN THE GOLD ROOM

The butter- fingered sun spills light
over daffodiled wallpaper;
flakes of gold foil peeling
like gilt from infinite domes.
So my room cannot be shabby
on days like this . . . the bright grain
of the hardwood floor warming
the feet on chilly mornings
as the malleable light spreads out,
turns this blue-shadowed bed linen
into warm yellow blankets
we can hide under.

Now the air hints of cedar
shavings, and I think of Norway:
the blond woodcarvers, porcelain
milkmaids with their bowls
of thick cream, and how
this spring morning is like
cold water sprinkled through
sunlight, as I cuddle
under covers, a sweetheart's
cool knees warming me
like rosy moons.

TASTING THE WINTER

It is so cold the air tastes like metal.
Not copper which is warm, but more like
steel, stained gun-metal blue. Then again
perhaps like nothing tangible at all,
just this astringent North Wind puckering
finger tips and membranes of the nose,
or filing across the edges of the teeth.
And so maybe there is no taste, only
the sense of something absent, tinctured
with the odor of hickory, which burns
in the fireplace before us as we drowse,
flames warming our toes after we have
skated all afternoon on the frozen pond.

Now, someone contemplates staying
home from school on a Monday morning
so that he might look out cozily with
one eye from under the covers. Half see
through frosted windows . . . those sugary,
ice-shelled trunks and branches clicking
brilliantly in the orange-juice sun.

AIR CONDITIONING

It puts us in the wrong place and time:
we no longer wake to bathe in the slow
steamy miasma which is August but
get out of bed swiftly, experience
this kind of quirky October.
Feet chilled by the bathroom tiles,
we wash and dress with a harried
agility, anticipating hot coffee,
the warm bacon and eggs, while outside
time runs heavy as the air,
and an old discomfort we remember
might almost seem welcome.

Now, closed up inside our house, we
wonder why things stay so much the same.
Not like as kids, when we heard
locusts droning a summer afternoon away,
could feel the approach of thunder
through open windows.
And later during the downpour,
quickened by the cool odor of rain
on hot concrete, we exploded outside
in just our swim suits,
splashed a path through the street
to an overflowing gutter . . .
bathed our thirsty feet in its rush.

FREAKS

My children surround me, all
vying for my attention, my love.
I slide my shoes away from them
trying to avoid contorted little
arms and legs, small leathery heads
like melons, the writhing trunks,
their strange juxtaposition of parts.

I tell them they must learn to stand
on their own two feet or whatever.
That I was like them once and look
at me now. (I laugh at this, sob
simultaneously behind my hand, under
my breath.) But they crowd around,
clutch at my trousers and coat, make
odd bleating noises from malformed
mouths and throats. I tell them to learn
to say their consonants and vowels,
find some kind of vocabulary, and
things might go better. Yet, I know
this is probably a lie. For with my
seething, ambidextrous cripples, no
hard-won elegance will make any
difference. Finally their words may
only define their own imperfection,
give well-shaped utterance to
what hurts them most to speak.

PROGENY

I never have enough time to make as many new ones
as I'd like. Lately I've been too busy tending to those
already here: calling in all the loiterers who were outside
playing tag, scuffling in the back alley, given them baths,
washed behind their ears, shampooed their matted hair,
laid out some clean, freshly-pressed clothes, and told
them to hurry up and get dressed . . . that pretty soon they
are to be sent out, presented to important company, stand
inspection before those who might make a real difference
                                        in their futures.

I do this wanting only the best for my offspring.
Yet I try to complete this business with a minimum
of effort, needing always to maintain my own vigor
and flow. Like on this very night (after the poems
are back, sweetly tucked-in, sound asleep on their
neat floppy disk) my Muse has been invited over
for dinner. And after our meal of rare meat and rarer
wine, some crazy talk in candlelight, she will perhaps
drag me up the stairs where I'll pull off her flimsy
white dress and together we'll make things really
                                        happen, again.

CONGRATULATING THE DEAD

Before the feast begins
we shall congratulate them
in their new gowns and tuxedos.
A formal ceremony will be given
with candles lit, medals presented
and a receiving line, grave
with smiles and rigid handshakes.
Then a high official shall present
keys to the city and music will
play while dancers sway stiffly
among the marble pillars.

Tables of cold meat shall then be
served along with expensive bitter
cordials from crystal decanters.
Nobody will notice flies
on the waxy hands.

THE DROWNED

*Divers found no human
remains in the wreck of Titanic.*

So many have lost their way
in the incomprehensible sea.
Even on the surface the surge
is duplicitous, while below
the myriad sand grains mock
with their identical faces.
On the journey between, fish
nose earlobes and skin
follicles. Corals wait to
imprint final bone with
their rough embroidery.

Dressed in the high fashion
of unraveling threads, they go
down . . . down, almost slipping
into glamorous poses as
salt fills interstitial spaces,
becomes their own tears.
And those who went before
greet their watery arrival
in hollow shrouds,
tiny waists . . . invisible.
Here, where these newly
fallen will finally settle, far
beneath the mirrored interface.
Here, where feet become
their own prints, and soft
dissolving hair just lifts up
toward the more open
sorrows of the waves.

MACHINE GUNNING THE ANGELS

They float by, always smiling . . .
cool, virtuous, spotlessly radiant.
I let each have a blast and
am a better shot than I thought.
Feathers and a silvery fluid
splatter in all directions.
After fifty consecutive bull's-eyes
I itch to hit the rest, when the
smoky pitchman abruptly appears
and with pale sweaty hands
nervously presents me the trophy.

There I stand, my arms
around it, a stuffed owl with
rotten stumps for wings,
a ridiculous grin
on the horny lips.

THE NEW ASSASSIN

I know them all except this new one,
a particularly ugly customer
with an oversized jaw and a beetled forehead,
wearing a bear coat heaved up
where he keeps his submachine gun
and afterdinner mints.
None manages to look like me but him
though they try, standing before a mirror
fingering their mustaches, nasal hairs,
and their .357 magnums in crotch holsters.
They make the Bronson smile,
the Bogart sneer, the mad Cagney
shriek, "Look at me, Ma, I'm
on top of the world!"

They corner me in the blind alley
of my hallway when I get up
at four in the morning to
go to the john.
But they all step aside when
this new one moves in, opens up
his coat and produces
his Uzi sub,
lets me have it with
his wintergreen smile.

DOWN THE NIGHT STAIRS

"It's always darkest before the dark," some
crazy guy told me once . . . once when I was
full of both arrogance and a bitter self-loathing.
And I thought I had misunderstood or misquoted
in my own dithery mania. And so I tried some
other combinations to try to get it straight and
finally found the old cliché, "It's always darkest
before the light." Now this seemed to me
the most absurd statement of all.

So maybe the crazy guy was right after all,
and I ought to interview someone else who might
know, like the poor fellow at the end of his rope.
Ask him three seconds before the stranger in
the suit of shadows has sprung the trap . . . then
after, through those bubbling blue lips, he might
have something important to say. Or ask
the one whose penis has just plopped out of
the slippery black hole two seconds before the
ultimate explosion. "What was it like?" I'd
say to his gnarled face, his fists clenched like
he might be prone to kill . . . and so move on
maybe a little quickly to his wanton partner
beneath him, she (of the rosy lips), who might
just consent to speak into my handy mike, gasp
a few heavy words maybe, or perhaps could
only scream, "Gravity, Gravity," like some
primal curse toward God.

And then I think of the efficacy of those early
scientific experiments trying to prove the existence
of the ether in the vacuum of space, and how light
bends around any attractive body and might be
displaced so no one is there when you look. And
suddenly I am back in my own underworld, a child
walking the twilight hall of his grandparents' house,
passing the constellation of empty doorways lined
up like vertical boxes along a corridor. Where later
at three in the morning between my mother and
father, I try very hard not to look down the night stairs,
where that awful white singularity peeks out, smiling
from the bottom, draws at my feet, pulling them
slowly back, back down toward some terrible
event-horizon, down to where real blackness begins.

DANDRUFF *ET AL.*

Dirt creeps in, more everyday: moles the
color of humus on the pale skin and this
soft grime under the fingernails. Have I
been digging in my backyard, and if so,
for what? Where are my familiar clean-cut
edges? The hair, what's left, is full of
insoluble snow: on my shoulders, the drift
of ancient blizzards has piled up in layers.
My once sharp image, defocused into a
bone-gray fuzzy figure, now plods, lurches
awkwardly into grim weather. And the once
keen sensorium numbs, the brightest colors
dim. Brilliance sublimates like shiny
iodine crystals or evaporates like cold
alcohol from a flaky scalp. From there
a fine dust, wafted by random air currents,
collects on shelves or becomes an oily
residue which darkens the blond oaken
corners of my desk. Not much longer now
till my backyard invites me back in, then a
final season of rain and softening, perhaps
. . . a lush new green topography of buds
and leaves sprouting from my black thumbs.

LUNAR DIARRHEA

When the moon is full so are you. And
so all the rest of the pack say you're sick,
full of it, and must go on a diet of radishes
and oatmeal, disdain cheeses and red meat.
Nobody wants to be full of it particularly
when out howling under a full moon, where
gleaming canines suddenly enlarge and hair
sprouts around both the palms of your hands
and soles of your feet . . . and the nails of the
digits sharpen and elongate and your ears
prick up and nose twitches to the scent of
perfume filtering through the graveyard.
Here, where you wait on all fours for the
loved one, she in her blue silk nightgown,
even now drifting across the dewy stones,
enduring the spiky manicured lawn, about
to become a partner in the hungry dance,
wanting your mouth across her translucent
throat, the deep bite to the heart when she
                        becomes yours forever.

You would not want to have an accident
at such a mythic moment like some
common Rover or Spot. Violate the dream,
so her mysterious smile goes suddenly awry
when snow white toes find the gooey mess
in the sweet damp grass. And then that awful
inappropriate gamy odor, and she (at once)
out of her trance, disgustedly heading back
to the dark house, leaving you to howl
and   bespatter   her
                    path   under   an
                            increasingly-
                                umber . . . . moon.

POEM WITH BIG FEET

This is the poem that walks
on big feet, that stomps on
all smaller poems, that says,
''get out of my way,'' when it
saunters through the barroom door.

This is the poem that interrupts
the conversation you are having with
your girlfriend and talks her into
dancing and then leaving without you,
so you must go home or dance by yourself.

This is the same poem which sits down
beside you the next day and eats all of
your french fries and wants a big bite
from your cheeseburger. That gives you
free advice about your terminal inadequacies
and offers you a gun, though it admits,
''this is the coward's way out.''

This is also the poem which tells you
that any greatness you might achieve
in this world is due to it, while
all failures are strictly your own.

This is the poem which is always
suffering because no one appreciates
its true merit, a poem that knows it
could have been a millionaire or an
important politician had it chosen
to be something else.

This is the poem I avoid trying
to write though it's always around
beating its chest, complaining,
intimidating the lyrical, quieter,
often deeper poems.

Still, because its feet are so big
and its space requirements enormous,
perhaps it can't help stomping on other
poems and things. Perhaps it is
not even cruel, just deprived:
having grown up without lessons
on the cello, and never enough
cheeseburgers on the backyard patio.

SPECIAL REPORT

My superiors are all on the phone energetically
reporting me to those in final authority.
They say there has been some drastic mistake in
my being sent here, that I am absolutely
useless at my station and sit here like a lump
doing nothing, that I am completely ignorant
of all the subtleties and grand purposes of
my profession (if that's what you call it). And
I have been taking credit for jobs even
the lowest yokel can perform with ease, but of
which (they are sure) I am completely incapable.
Thus I have fattened on bread I've never properly
earned, and even the clothing on my back is
rightly the property of others. And so any
happiness or sense of security which I might feel is
altogether unmerited and worthy only of contempt
. . . that somebody, the stars perhaps, should
send down their wrath, and the wonderful sunsets
of which I'm so fond be changed before my eyes
into bloody suppurating sores, that I be made to see
and sense my guilt by viewing my body from
the *inside* only: these thickening arteries and veins,
the stench of my decaying entrails, the disgusting
liquescence of my tissues. They say I should
never have been permitted to rise from the slime
of which I am such an intractable part.

And thus it is clear to all and must be made clear
to me that I was never meant for here: for sunlight
or starlight, not for clear air or even the rain.
That, for me, evolution was a mistake
and I should still be oozing between rocks
at the bottom of some murky and pestilent sea.

HOLY COW!

The sanctimonious always tether their bovines high, closer
to heaven for grazing. Maybe on tops of skyscrapers, roof-
gardens of famous padres of industry. Here, a carnal yet
ineffectual piety tugs at the teats leaving meager pools of
milk in the cereal bowls of pet wives and familial wolverines
(all those of a similar digestive cramp). Below, the markets
still bull and bear along, for no one hardly remembers when
their great-grandfathers climbed up here, walked on air, and
so relieved themselves of sore feet, forever. Above this very
city, where the wind now conducts its mysterious orchestra,
while down in the cafes, couples dance to the newest craze
they call "the Nada," after the Goddess of Nothing. (For when
they press close enough together, they pass through each other
without even touching and thus maintain a dry desire behind
their turgid yet frozen spigots.)

And so everyone scrapes up all the green stuff they can out
in the countryside, which they hoard, though it changes to a
fine gray powder inside their chromium vaults. Found along
the highways it is always being replaced by mall after mall
anyway, which they are sure God would have made Himself
if He'd had an extra day or two. "So much overtime," every-
one exclaims, "but someone's got to do it. After all, only the
work makes us free." We say this over and over as we idly
diddle along the aisles of the supermarket in search for aci-
dophilus milk and guava fruit. Spread our green cheeks over
the checkout counter while admiring the great metal dugs on
the chest of the robot cashier.

CAVEAT

It is not a good idea to scorn Mr. Scornoff,
Scornoff with his gray metastasizing leg.

It is not a good idea, a good idea, as he comes
down the stair in his pantaloons and festering smile,

carrying his rectal-linear, ice-cold silver egg,
it is not a good idea, a good idea.

For the avuncular Mr. Scornoff can become extremely vile
with his nicotine hand and red-cracked parchment eye

and his shiny dentist's pliers that can be slipped right in
just between the most sensitive bones and skin.

It is not a good idea to scorn the scorpulous Mr. Scornoff.
Scornoff, with his mucid self-fertilizing style,

with his organo-sulfur stench and velveteen bag
caked with sticky crystals and blood-black gamy bile,

unmentionable remnants of what was once contained within.
Even the flies would avoid the carious Scornoff

but cannot, cannot. They are raisins drawn to Scornoff's
eye and he picks them off like scaly fruit

to garnish his favorite dish of ripened "road-kill-opossum",
which he consumes by the gallon, by the gallon.

And the waiters would all like to run but will not, as
they cater to Scornoff's needs by the bucket, by the bucket.

They will not scorn Mr. Scornoff, who leaves his sodden tip
in a pool of drool and slavered gall.

For it is just not a good thing to scorn Mr. Scornoff,
not a wise idea at all.

AN OLD STORY

The cave is always with us: the
hirsute brain scratching viciously
against its walls. When strangers
see stony epaulets decking our
brutish shoulders, they run, terrified
. . . and we after them, determined
to grind them up, to take possession of
their women, allow no surviving sons.

Today we resolve that no one,
particularly ourselves, will know
our vile predilections, the cor-
rosive vanity we feed upon
as we say anything to make
others the despots of our story.
Draw a protective circle around
ourselves with their blood . . .
sit safe before a sooty flame
sharpening flints, muttering
always of even more outrageous
depredations, some newer klatch
of maggots hatched
by a haughty and tyrannical sun.

ON THE DEATH OF CLOCKS

One day they'll die, you know.
Swallow their pendulums and choke,
coughing up chimes and gears,
hands going around backwards
then forwards
and finally hanging loose,
dangling over six o'clock
from the center post.
And the electric clocks
(even digitals) will fry,
fizzle, disgorging their quartz
crystals, flashing, giving off
sparks, tears streaming down
dials and faces, when
everything will fuse
into one lump of
cooked metal, plastic
and wires.

And then the sun will stop,
confused,
for no one will tell it
where to go.
And the shadows will freeze,
and the wind become quiet,
and the water drops from
the fountain will stay
in the air, and the swan
on the lake won't move
a feather,
and it will be perfect,

like a postcard I got
from Zurich
seven years ago.

SHOES

Tonight before this dog-weary fire I
recount the terrible history of my shoes,
how for over four years they have
accompanied me everywhere.
Gone through the worst the streets
have had to offer,
the frivolities and nightmares
of my life.
How my shoes have been faithful always,
maybe more so than my feet
that are given to complaining about
the toes and sometimes the sensitive
bone of the left heel.
My shoes, I repeat, followed me everywhere
like a squire or poodle or the fans
of a rock musician, without contention
or one mean squeak.

Now over the last months I have
noticed, alas, that they have finally
begun their decline.
The tongues no longer have their
former wit and the eyes
are bleary from seeing too many ankles,
and worse still, both soles have cracked.
They have become a pair of old men
with bad teeth, whose mouths
have begun to smell.
For when I sit and cross my legs
so my shoes are almost at face level
with my friends,
I notice how everyone turns away
or gets up and leaves the room.

I have tried changing socks
three times a day
but the condition seems irreversible.
And though my shoes are still
for the most part very comfortable,
there is sometimes a cool shock
when I go to the restroom
of my favorite dive.
Where many, after drinking much,
have found the floor more accessible
than the overflowing convenience on the wall.
Or after hours when I make my way
through the whirling parking lot
and there is something yellow-orange
and grossly sour and slippery
on the bottoms of my shoes,
I know the cracks in the soles
will sop it all up to my toes.
Poor shoes no longer able to defend
me or themselves
when I walk in long dappled grass
of the park and must
be extremely careful of those
rich greener patches . . .
traps laid by cunning dogs.

But what can I do? I can't just
throw them away or send them
to a nursing home, or burn them
(God forbid); they have been too faithful.
Yet when I enter a room
I know everyone is looking down
at them in disgust
and then up at me as if saying,
"do something with them."

And when I go to bed they look
up at me sadly
as if they expected to be beaten
for no fault of their own.
Then I know I must relieve them
of their burden, hide them
from their persecutors,
those who would reward fidelity
with betrayal.
I know one day I might be
like them:
no longer of any use,
collecting dust and dog hair,
cowering perpetually
under the bed.

SEVEN PROSE POEMS

I   *Of The Judges*

One day it occurs to me just how much one is celebrated for every worthless deed he or she has done and that some deeds are not only worthless but actually evil. The judges, who rattle the cages we all live in, really enjoy this since it presents a real spectacle. For the average judge evil is a spectacular because it usually produces colors: red mostly, but sometimes blue or purple in its greater depths. And what really amazes is that these deeds so clothe themselves that they might appear as something with real value or even as an act which is intrinsically good. The judges really love that for then they can stretch their fingers eerily into the air and pretend to be playing gold strings which make sweet rapturous music even though anyone with sense knows gold strings can hardly make any musical sounds, gold being so soft and ductile that it cannot sustain tension and so the strings would pull away from their pegs. But the judges don't care, they know a good thing when the proper person tells them so. They have this kind of seventh sense which is present only when they are being briefed by someone of great authority, then of course, they know how to re-echo with sonorous effect.

Now everyone has an opinion and those most guilty have the most excuses and so may have a very sound case or at least one with many opinions and options. Then a real judge can make decisions and fly around all day in an expensive car telling people to get out of his way while he strums his lute (without gold strings if the judge has a modicum of sense), and though a good or honorable act may have no excuses *at all* and so exist only on the frivolousness of the air or the glow of a sunset or moonrise. A good act like love is where one is taken in on a large, soft, flower-scented mattress with satin sheets and many extra pillows, even when the object of that love has no apparent redeeming quality, but is only a vision in someone else's eyes, of their own need-to-be-completed self. So what, that that person might have a fine singing voice and manufacture handsome bird cages in his or her leisure hours. Still that person is nearly always a deficient being. Who, if observed closely, would just about reflect the admirer tit-for-tat, and so, as even a mediocre judge might observe, come to union carnally congruent but no closer to perfection.

II   *An Irradiant Muse*

You're really a dangerous man Mr. "A." So pure in your conversation that the human condition rarely touches your syllables. And so you go on and on and we all follow because we are having such a good time. Almost like seeing an early Bergman film or an MGM musical again after all these years, not a hint of any real substance, thank heavens. No real sewage pipes leading into the bountiful blue Baltic, no waste lumps falling frozen from the beautiful calligraphic contrails of jets skimming the high autumn air. And even if you included them, as one day you almost certainly will, there would be a transmogrification. You cannot help it that you're so unequivocal and thus dangerous. You stand in a strange light and say your decocted epigrams to fractured shadows and both the earthworms and coffin worms pop up to see what's cooking in your garden. Or maybe you take us to Rio or Madrid or even to Vienna to check out Freud's couch and Schubert's piano, then maybe to Rappaccini's garden (but no . . . that must be in Italy, Rome or Florence perhaps). Wasn't Hawthorne an ambassador there or something? But the Italianate name is quite inconsequential anyway, as the setting has enough of your own Gothic ambiance.

After all wouldn't everyone really enjoy a full-blooded vampire dressed in a fine midnight-blue tuxedo with a red satin ribbon stretched across the immaculate starched white front just like some ambassador to a fabled Carpathian kingdom (or would it be in the Caucasus or Harz) playing the Saint-Saens' fourth piano concerto in C minor (last movement) on a huge Bösendorfer while outside the snow is falling, and all at ten o'clock P.M. on a Christmas Eve? There of course, along with myself, the blue children would be listening, rubbing their hands together in the bitter cold, held by the music that filters through stained-glass windows and by the indelible conversation of poems caught in the windy pines. One would know then, that March was imminent even at this early date, and that the pain of being alive was slowly diffusing back into the blanched limbs. So it is a sorry state for us, that you, "A," the *charge d'affaires*, cannot keep this rich illuminated image before us, allow us to watch unchallenged from these frost-rimed battlements . . . forever.

III   *Blue*

What pleased me most was her cool quality, like laundry starch, or the blueing that used to be soaked into white shirts, and the smell of bleach helped but also could be overdone which raised the temp a bit and I really enjoyed "cool" the best. Like in the lap of this modest young woman where I would lay my head (not too young, maybe in her middle- to late-whatevers and just innocent enough not even to realize her own innocence as she planted cornflowers and sweet pea in the window boxes and in the margins of the backyard or under the window air conditioner). So tall-stemmed, she, and soap-fresh, and as unassuming as a flower, completely oblivious of the gifts she had to offer.

And so she was like that and a perfect metaphor for whatever I was chiefly talking about before she presented her lovely presence. Those others with their ripe curved forms, pungent like that first real spring breeze in spring and/or (paradoxically) like that first hint of autumn in the late summer light, a browning of the gray summer shadows long before the first blue frost, a soft smoke-like essence in the fading heat. And that summer sidewalk I remember on my bare feet just as the sun was going down, the warm texture in such blissful contact . . . cool by contrast with the hot August noon. And the sky to the North, I could dote on that forever, the way it hung over the earth, over this infinite island. The still-point, 40 degrees up from where I stood surrounded by the horizon's rim, blue as an enameled metal cup ready for well water or rain, or thinking again of hot, sweet, amber drinks in the frost of the waning year, held up to the color of rose before the season's early night, and then again back to that real figure in her garden, the freshening wind, the rich blue eye of the North, summer/winter somehow combined: the spring, the fall, all of the same equation so you could take either side or ride the middle. Know the perfection of imperfect balance as she settles closer to you (you still a boy), this woman now a girl in a blue cornflower dress imprinting her taut new body against the side of the still impressionable wind.

IV *Extravagance As The Measure Of Futility And Ambition*

Secure yourself a sinecure if you want to be happy, maybe somewhere between the heavy pages of a book on Prediluvian Phrenology or even flat-out on the cover of some Danish porno pulp. None of the subtleties are really necessary as long as you supply the proper incentives to the Governor, the President or maybe even to the doorman (in France, a *concierge* if they're not all extinct). But space it wide anyhow, anything in two dimensions automatically stands a better chance. Don't try to raise up or push down. The doors will all still be closed and it would be too humorous to contemplate your own reflection inside a brass elevator (everyone would laugh, even you, if you could step outside yourself and visualize the scene).

But if a sinecure is out of the question (and one certainly would be troubled by any other substitute, even by a sycamore) then something plainer might suffice. Maybe something purchased from Joe Bogma's clock tower out there in the middle of the woods behind the noodle factory, the place where Joe was employed for many years before he discovered his enormous talent in chronologistics. No matter that the woods are mined and synchronized. This was done merely as an afterthought after the flood receded, when there was some need for aeration of the soil, and being the practical people that they were, the inhabitants sought the help of one who until only recently had been one of them. One, who had dangled noodles with the worst, over the anhydrous sulfur pits, who had sat in on their games of "crump" during the breaks and first dabbled there in self-frenetics. But he was at his best (doing it particularly well) when underwater or under the spell of Fangour, his pet Quetzal which he had found while parsing the tops of those Gingko trees he had planted in concentric circles around his former habitat. And so everyone was satisfied that his performances were not mere show but based on that naturally directed achronistacy which he had probably been born with.

Nosiree, I don't think there are any more indirect roads to happiness than this. Still the sycamores are fast growing, true, and have many face-sized leaves which can be used as wallpaper when not glued to your inside terminals or hooked to the external ear sockets via the leathery bark slivers. Getting back to nature is, I suppose, what it's all about anyway. And doesn't nature offer us a sinecure even when mined by explosives? And isn't the exploitation of time the only game we are all involved in, whether we like it or not? Anyhow in such a short interval as our lives are, the doors cannot possibly be opened or closed, not by all the elevator repairmen in China.

V   *Morte D'Arthur*

Forget the anecdotes and anagrams, the caustics and acrostics, the sticky fingers on the chessmen, on the Queen herself (Heaven forbid, who would have conceived such a violation?), and she only trying to protect the King. The Black Knight, that scoundrel, such obvious concupiscence under his steel-plated codpiece. This print from a block grooved out by the fine hand of a medieval artisan in the south of France. And the whole episode falling between the rounds of a tournament (a play within a play, one might say: Guinevere with her thin enigmatic smile, her hand on Arthur's member under the tablecloth but all the while her longing glance burning into Lancelot, for she knew he had a lot of what she wanted most, had seen him bathing nude in the lake and polishing it up for the likes of "Elaine the Fair" or some other maiden in dire distress, vibrators not having been invented yet and there being no batteries or A.C. outlets in this period of history, anyway).

And so the horns echo in the distance, through the ancient checkered valleys, and as to a call of arms all the engines turn over, the armatures twisting through their magnetic fields as the backhoes and bulldozers move in, while computers spew their menus and estimates between glass lips of an overflowing monitor. Then the "Ladies of the Court" slip into their cheerleading costumes and undulate into the arena straddling pompoms and the necks of quarterbacks. Around the lake an uninterrupted file of Hondas, Chevrolets, and Fords nose the rears of their metallic companions, while in the center of the lake, beneath its flocculent depths, embedded in a rank pile of garbage, the sword Excalibur rusts beside the fender of a blue '69 Buick.

VI *Discontinuity*

The magician, who cuts the rope with the scissors, mutters an incantation then gestures mysteriously while his beautiful assistant watches in her sparkly G-string. Then he passes the rope around her waist, gives a stout tug and the rope miraculously heels, follows the magician with little yips of pleasure and excitement into the wings.

Later Whizzaro, for that is his stage name, helps his assistant, Diapassia, into an oblong box, opens a case containing the shiny new rip-saw with its red mahogany handle. Then he closes the box which encases all but head and feet of the lovely woman, centers the saw about halfway between chin and knee and saws away for about two-and-a-half minutes. When the audience begins to hear a difference in the quality of the sound, the magician too notices that the teeth seem to have bitten into something more than just highly-lacquered pine. It is then that the woman starts to breathe hard and sigh, cry out as if engulfed by some sensual pleasure which only intensifies with each new stroke of the saw. At this the magician becomes enraged, pulls the saw from its newly-manufactured slot and throws it angrily to the floor of the stage. He opens the box and is at first astounded by what he sees, then leaps into it full length, grabs the inner handle of the lid and pulls it down on top of both him and his lady. With this there is a sudden flash and momentary darkness followed by the utter disappearance of both couple and box.

On the backdrop behind the stage a crescent moon is painted floating against a cloud-plopped sky, followed by the figure of an inflamed amorous pink cow in the act of making a grand leap over the moon's horn. In the front row a little old lady laughs to see such sport, while the saw (after picking itself up off the stage, brushing off the sawdust and other debris) runs away with the scissors.

VII *Against The Collapse Of Indigenous Indigoes*

They were there to begin with and so we need not trouble ourselves too much with history . . . unless of course, we wish to. And while the progress of the project may depend a lot upon our own good taste or our lack thereof, still the whole thing could be really very thrilling . . . to think of the depths to which we would have to plummet and once there the beauty, the subtlety, these adamantine plains refracting all of those saturated colors. Like feathers of a very black bird, plucked out and held at some oblique angle to the sunlight or if that isn't available, to some other more permanent and furious source. Something perhaps found at the core of each of our own individual cells or at the center of a crystal, though I am not talking of some molecular or atomic array, particularly. Only saying, almost coincidentally, that these would be very attractive signposts, something to tantalize us along the way.

But speaking of the journey (and I know this is one of the most attractive aspects of the quest), there might be other less excursive methods to achieve our aims, methods more straightforward, more economical and in the end more conducive to success. Sight is such a wonderful gift: we need not always run up to the thing itself, to taste it or feel. Even at a distance the image may engrain itself on the retina with such intensity that it could reveal all we want to know or need to experience. Yet to smell the perfume, touch the fascinating surface, saturate ourselves with both the ambiance or clarity of the thing, its marvelous shades, the stippling in its shadowed areas, the colors that stain our fingers, the soles of our feet, even the sleeves of our cassocks. (Oh yes, for we must all approach these multi-gloried levels dressed in the proper habit, and in the right habit of mind if we are to take in the glow.) We must also be aware of that fragility which our own presence will only contribute to, and know the gifts which are most precious to us have always been those which dissolve to nothing as we reach out to grasp. And so we must keep our hands close to our bodies, be both proud and humble but most of all thankful for this slippery ledge on which our feet are so precariously placed. Knowing that a fall could not only maim or destroy ourselves but distort that fine complexity we have come so far to experience, and for which we were born to see.

ABOUT THE AUTHOR

Richard Pflum is a native of Indianapolis, Indiana. He is the author of a full-length book of poetry, *A Dream of Salt*, 1980, and the chapbook *Moving Into the Light*, 1975, both with the Raintree Press (now called the Fred Brewer Press) of Bloomington, Indiana. In his workaday life Pflum has engaged in such diverse occupations as: teaching in the public schools (math and science), working as a photographer, as a writer-in-the-schools, teaching part-time in college (beginning creative writing), and as a lab attendant on a biochemical research team. He is currently a psychiatric attendant in a state mental hospital and leads a poetry interest group through the Writers' Center of Indianapolis. He feels that the broad experience of a life teaches that time is the only significant dimension, and that the best education for a poet is to know as much as possible about everything. And so, though there are limitations for every human being, one must never believe it.